TRUST IN THE LORD WITH
ALL YOUR HEART
AND LEAN NOT ON YOUR
OWN UNDERSTANDING;
IN ALL YOUR WAYS SUBMIT
TO HIM
AND HE WILL MAKE YOUR
PATHS STRAIGHT

Proverbs 3:5-6

Printed by CreateSpace, An Amazon.com Company

Date: _____

My Requests:

Bible Verse:

My Prayer:

Answers:

Thank You, Lord For...

Date: _____

My Requests:

Bible Verse:

My Prayer:

Answers:

Thank You, Lord For...

Date: _____

My Requests:

Bible Verse:

My Prayer:

Answers:

Thank You, Lord For...

Date: _____

My Requests:

Bible Verse:

My Prayer:

Answers:

Thank You, Lord For...

Date: _____

My Requests:

Bible Verse:

My Prayer:

Answers:

Thank You, Lord For...

Date: _____

My Requests:

Bible Verse:

My Prayer:

Answers:

Thank You, Lord For...

Date: _____

My Requests:

Bible Verse:

My Prayer:

Answers:

Thank You, Lord For...

Date: _____

My Requests:

Bible Verse:

My Prayer:

Answers:

Thank You, Lord For...

Date: _____

My Requests:

Bible Verse:

My Prayer:

Answers:

Thank You, Lord For...

Date: _____

My Requests:

Bible Verse:

My Prayer:

Answers:

Thank You, Lord For...

Date: _____

My Requests:

Bible Verse:

My Prayer:

Answers:

Thank You, Lord For...

Date: _____

My Requests:

Bible Verse:

My Prayer:

Answers:

Thank You, Lord For...

Date: _____

My Requests:

Bible Verse:

My Prayer:

Answers:

Thank You, Lord For...

Date: _____

My Requests:

Bible Verse:

My Prayer:

Answers:

Thank You, Lord For...

Date: _____

My Requests:

Bible Verse:

My Prayer:

Answers:

Thank You, Lord For...

Date: _____

My Requests:

Bible Verse:

My Prayer:

Answers:

Thank You, Lord For...

Date: _____

My Requests:

Bible Verse:

My Prayer:

Answers:

Thank You, Lord For...

Date: _____

My Requests:

Bible Verse:

My Prayer:

Answers:

Thank You, Lord For...

Date: _____

My Requests:

Bible Verse:

My Prayer:

Answers:

Thank You, Lord For...

Date: _____

My Requests:

Bible Verse:

My Prayer:

Answers:

Thank You, Lord For...

Date: _____

My Requests:

Bible Verse:

My Prayer:

Answers:

Thank You, Lord For...

Date: _____

My Requests:

Bible Verse:

My Prayer:

Answers:

Thank You, Lord For...

Date: _____

My Requests:

Bible Verse:

My Prayer:

Answers:

Thank You, Lord For...

Date: _____

My Requests:

Bible Verse:

My Prayer:

Answers:

Thank You, Lord For...

Date: _____

My Requests:

Bible Verse:

My Prayer:

Answers:

Thank You, Lord For...

Date: _____

My Requests:

Bible Verse:

My Prayer:

Answers:

Thank You, Lord For...

Date: _____

My Requests:

Bible Verse:

My Prayer:

Answers:

Thank You, Lord For...

Date: _____

My Requests:

Bible Verse:

My Prayer:

Answers:

Thank You, Lord For...

Date: _____

My Requests:

Bible Verse:

My Prayer:

Answers:

Thank You, Lord For...

Date: _____

My Requests:

Bible Verse:

My Prayer:

Answers:

Thank You, Lord For...

Date: _____

My Requests:

Bible Verse:

My Prayer:

Answers:

Thank You, Lord For...

Date: _____

My Requests:

Bible Verse:

My Prayer:

Answers:

Thank You, Lord For...

Date: _____

My Requests:

Bible Verse:

My Prayer:

Answers:

Thank You, Lord For...

Date: _____

My Requests:

Bible Verse:

My Prayer:

Answers:

Thank You, Lord For...

Date: _____

My Requests:

Bible Verse:

My Prayer:

Answers:

Thank You, Lord For...

Date: _____

My Requests:

Bible Verse:

My Prayer:

Answers:

Thank You, Lord For...

Date: _____

My Requests:

Bible Verse:

My Prayer:

Answers:

Thank You, Lord For...

Date: _____

My Requests:

Bible Verse:

My Prayer:

Answers:

Thank You, Lord For...

Date: _____

My Requests:

Bible Verse:

My Prayer:

Answers:

Thank You, Lord For...

Date: _____

My Requests:

Bible Verse:

My Prayer:

Answers:

Thank You, Lord For...

Date: _____

My Requests:

Bible Verse:

My Prayer:

Answers:

Thank You, Lord For...

Date: _____

My Requests:

Bible Verse:

My Prayer:

Answers:

Thank You, Lord For...

Date: _____

My Requests:

Bible Verse:

My Prayer:

Answers:

Thank You, Lord For...

Date: _____

My Requests:

Bible Verse:

My Prayer:

Answers:

Thank You, Lord For...

Date: _____

My Requests:

Bible Verse:

My Prayer:

Answers:

Thank You, Lord For...

Date: _____

My Requests:

Bible Verse:

My Prayer:

Answers:

Thank You, Lord For...

Date: _____

My Requests:

Bible Verse:

My Prayer:

Answers:

Thank You, Lord For...

Date: _____

My Requests:

Bible Verse:

My Prayer:

Answers:

Thank You, Lord For...

Date: _____

My Requests:

Bible Verse:

My Prayer:

Answers:

Thank You, Lord For...

Date: _____

My Requests:

Bible Verse:

My Prayer:

Answers:

Thank You, Lord For...

Date: _____

My Requests:

Bible Verse:

My Prayer:

Answers:

Thank You, Lord For...

Date: _____

My Requests:

Bible Verse:

My Prayer:

Answers:

Thank You, Lord For...

Date: _____

My Requests:

Bible Verse:

My Prayer:

Answers:

Thank You, Lord For...

Date: _____

My Requests:

Bible Verse:

My Prayer:

Answers:

Thank You, Lord For...

Date: _____

My Requests:

Bible Verse:

My Prayer:

Answers:

Thank You, Lord For...

Date: _____

My Requests:

Bible Verse:

My Prayer:

Answers:

Thank You, Lord For...

Date: _____

My Requests:

Bible Verse:

My Prayer:

Answers:

Thank You, Lord For...

Date: _____

My Requests:

Bible Verse:

My Prayer:

Answers:

Thank You, Lord For...

Date: _____

My Requests:

Bible Verse:

My Prayer:

Answers:

Thank You, Lord For...

Date: _____

My Requests:

Bible Verse:

My Prayer:

Answers:

Thank You, Lord For...

Date: _____

My Requests:

Bible Verse:

My Prayer:

Answers:

Thank You, Lord For...

Date: _____

My Requests:

Bible Verse:

My Prayer:

Answers:

Thank You, Lord For...

Date: _____

My Requests:

Bible Verse:

My Prayer:

Answers:

Thank You, Lord For...

Date: _____

My Requests:

Bible Verse:

My Prayer:

Answers:

Thank You, Lord For...

Date: _____

My Requests:

Bible Verse:

My Prayer:

Answers:

Thank You, Lord For...

Date: _____

My Requests:

Bible Verse:

My Prayer:

Answers:

Thank You, Lord For...

Made in United States
Troutdale, OR
02/05/2024

17462822R00075